ROADS Publishing
149 Lower Baggot Street
Dublin 2
Ireland

www.roads.co

First published 2017

1

Marrakech: The Considered Guide

All of the businesses herein were chosen at the discretion of the publishers.
No payments or incentives were offered or received to ensure inclusion.

Art direction by
Alessio Avventuroso

Designed by
Agenzia del Contemporaneo

Printed in Italy by
Grafiche Damiani – Faenza Group SpA

978-1-909399-95-2

Marrakech

The Considered Guide

Growing up, travel was a major part of my life. It was and remains an integral source of education and inspiration. When I travel, I actively search out the most interesting and innovative places. As a rule, I ask my friends and contacts in each city for a list of their favourite places. I then keep and share with others my lists of places both recommended and those I discovered myself. Therefore, I decided to create the kind of travel guide that I myself would find useful: a carefully edited selection of the best places in a city – a book that is practical, beautiful, and, crucially, trustworthy.

The Considered Guide reflects the desires of the discerning traveller who cares deeply about how they spend their valuable time and money, and who appreciates impeccable service, beautiful design and attention to detail at every price level.

I am proud to say that I visited each and every place in this guide, and can vouch for the quality of each of them as personal recommendations.

Danielle Ryan
Founder of ROADS

Introduction

Set against the backdrop of the majestic Atlas Mountains, Marrakech is a singular destination; a melting pot of influences and experiences that combines East and West, tradition and modern glamour, vitality and serenity. Home to just under 1 million people, it welcomes over 8 million visitors per year, who are drawn to this city of contrasts.

Marrakech is commonly known as the 'Ochre City', due to its sandstone architecture and extensive city walls that were constructed in the twelfth century. While this soothing hue dominates, everywhere you turn there are bursts of colour. Indeed, the legendary fashion designer Yves Saint Laurent, who was to form an intense bond with the city, said, 'A visit to Marrakech was a great shock to me. This city taught me colour.'

This area had been inhabited by Berber farmers since Neolithic times, but in 1062 the city of Marrakech was established by Sultan Youssef ben Tachfine, under whose direction numerous important buildings were constructed and the city experienced massive prosperity. Its importance in Morocco gradually dwindled, but was reinvigorated in the sixteenth century under the Arabian Saadian dynasty. The early twentieth century saw the establishment of the French Protectorate, and although Morocco regained its independence in 1956, the influence of their former colonisers is still evident throughout the city. From around the mid-1960s, Marrakech gained a reputation as a hippie haven, and luminaries like the Rolling Stones and Jimi Hendrix descended upon the city to experience its heady delights, thus establishing a lasting connection between the city and the A-list.

The city itself can be broadly divided into the ancient Medina and the Ville Nouvelle. The Medina is encircled by almost 20km of 9-metre high walls, and it is here that you will find the majority of ancient landmarks. With its narrow streets and bustling atmosphere, exploring the Medina is a unique joy; you're bound to get lost at least once, but that is all part of the experience. The huge Jemaa el-Fnaa square is the heart of the Medina, and the city in general; all day long it is thronged with vendors, performers and those looking to entertain tourists at a price, and at night the carnival atmosphere intensifies. The northern edge of Djemma el-Fnaa leads you to the amazing souks, a mass of meandering pinkish streets teeming with stalls selling crafts, clothing and souvenirs. Historically, it was here that the caravans would congregate to trade their wares, and it remains a vital, vibrant part of the city, employing some 40,000 people.

The Ville Nouvelle, in contrast, was built by French colonial settlers in the early twentieth century and retains much of its art nouveau flavour. Highlights of this area include the downtown district of Gueliz, with its wide avenues lined with contemporary boutiques and cafés, and Hivernage, once the embassy district and now home to upmarket hotels, bars and clubs. As a predominantly Muslim city, there isn't the same drinking culture that you might find in Europe, but the ever-growing tourist industry has seen rules relaxed. Alcohol is available in exclusive venues in the Medina, but the Nouvelle Ville offers plenty of licensed nightlife options, even during Ramadan.

These two sides of Marrakech offer differing styles of accommodation; the city's slick modern hotels loom large in the Ville Nouvelle, whereas in the Medina classic riads are more common. A riad is a traditional Moroccan house with an interior courtyard, and there are over one thousand in Marrakech. A lot of those in the Medina have been lovingly converted into guesthouses, and these are pure oases of calm in the frenetic old town, many with roof terraces and private hammams (steam rooms similar to Turkish baths).

The current King, Mohammed VI, has invested heavily in asserting Morocco as a world leader in culture, and with the Marrakech Biennale and the Film Festival growing year upon year, even more people are being drawn to the Ochre City.

It is perhaps a cliché to call Marrakech a feast for all the senses, but with its rich cuisine, excellent shopping, thriving nightlife and friendly population, it truly is just that. A beguiling blend of tradition and modernity that's propelled by local craft and culture, few cities can offer as much variety as Marrakech; at once relaxing and energising, it is an ideal destination that guarantees a magical, memorable experience.

Marrakech has a reputation for being difficult to negotiate, but despite its size, and the labyrinthine souks, it's not really too hard to navigate. It is best to explore the Medina on foot; it is almost certain that you will get lost at least once, but that is part of the fun. It is highly recommended that you have GPS on your phone that you can use without mobile data. In general, hotels are very helpful, both in terms of advising on best transport options and, in the case of those within the Medina, in accompanying you to difficult-to-find places, such as restaurants and bars. Longer journeys may seem manageable on foot but can prove tricky and tiring in hot temperatures, so buses or taxis are a good way to preserve your energy for the job of exploring. It is advisable to brief yourself on what taxis should cost, as overcharging or adding dubious fees is common. As ever, haggling over prices is expected.

Getting around

From the airport

The airport is very conveniently located, just 5km from the city centre. The air-conditioned Number 19 airport bus runs every half hour from approximately 6am to 9.30pm; a single ticket costs 30 Dhs and the bus goes to Jemaa el-Fnaa and onwards to Gueliz. If you prefer to travel by taxi, you must agree on a price before getting into the car, as drivers are notorious for inflating prices. Avoid the taxis at the door of the terminal, and enquire with the more dependable drivers across the carpark. A daytime trip to the Medina should not cost more than 80 Dhs.

Taxis

There are two types of taxis in Marrakech, petite taxis and grand taxis. Petite taxis can carry three people and charge according to the meter, whereas the larger grand taxis can carry six and are charged as per a pre-agreed price. Grand taxis are typically engaged for longer journeys, so petite taxis are more common for zipping around the city. A ten-minute journey should cost you around 20 Dhs; ensure that the meter is used.

Buses

alsa.ma

There is a good local bus network, operated by Alsa, with services every fifteen to twenty minutes from around 6am to 10pm. Almost all of them stop at Jemaa el-Fnaa and tickets cost around 4 Dhs, which you pay to the driver when you board. Typically, these buses are busy and very warm, so they're best for short journeys.

Bicycle

Travelling by bicycle is a fun and memorable way to experience the city. The terrain is flat and in the Medina in particular a lot of streets are inaccessible to traffic; expect lots of bell ringing and emergency stops as you work your way through the maze-like streets. You can rent a bike for around 120 Dhs per day; be sure to use a legitimate firm with proof of insurance.

Calèches

Calèches are horse-drawn carriages that can be hired at Pl de Foucauld next to the Jemaa el-Fnaa for a fixed rate of 120 Dhs per hour (but you should still agree a price before boarding). There are three hundred calèches in the city, and while it is not the speediest mode of transportation, it is certainly a romantic way to tour the city.

Hotels

Amanjena

€€€€

Amanjena is a remarkable hotel 12km south of Marrakech that encompasses thirty-two pavilions (each with a private courtyard) and seven mansions (multi-level suites with individual pools and gardens). The complex is the work of architect Ed Tuttle, who set about creating his vision of a Moorish–Arabian paradise, and the design of the resort perfectly integrates the mature olive and date trees on the property. The network of suites allows visitors as much privacy or interaction as they desire; meals can be taken privately in your mansion, in the elegant restaurant, in the relaxed izakaya, or by candlelight in the caidal tent. Add to this an excellent spa and breathtaking views, and Amanjena is in every aspect the 'peaceful paradise' its name suggests.

—

Route de Ouarzazate Km 12, Marrakech 40000
aman.com/resorts/amanjena
+212 5243-99000

Dar Seven

This bijou luxury riad was recently converted by owner Principessa Letizia Ruspoli, whose attention to detail and focus on exquisite service have quickly made a name for Dar Seven. It is located in the Medina, and when you have navigated the alleyways you are rewarded with a breath of fresh air as a bright white courtyard welcomes you. There are just four rooms, but the interiors are contemporary and airy, lending it a truly relaxing atmosphere, and it's crowned with a rooftop terrace that has views of the Atlas Mountains. Breakfasts are good, and the staff are extremely attentive; they are happy to organise mobile phones (it can be extremely expensive to use a European phone), the use of a nearby swimming pool, or to lead you to and from taxi points.

€€

—

7 Derb Ben Moussa, Kaa Sour, Sidi Benslimane, Marrakech 40000
darseven.com
+212 5243-76753

Ksar Char-Bagh

€€€

Ksar Char-Bagh was built as recently as 2003, but it has already been named amongst the world's most beautiful hotels six times. The architecture was inspired by the Alhambra in Granada, and it is imbued with a sense of tranquil elegance. There are fifteen suites, seven with private terraces, a hammam, a cosy library bar and a stunning Spanish-style orangerie hall for indoor dining in inclement weather. Although young, the gardens are beautifully developed and maintained. There are lush green lawns, and a herb garden, fig trees and olive trees producing ingredients for Antoine Gonzalez's wonderful Mediterranean cooking. A peaceful escape from the chaos of the city, the hotel is located 6km from the Medina, and there is a driver on call for your convenience.

—

Djnan Abiad, La Palmeraie B.P. 12478, 40000 Marrakech
ksarcharbagh.fr
+212 5243-29244

Palais Rhoul

The five-star Palais Rhoul is situated in the popular Palmeraie district to the north of the city. The hotel's main building is a work of art; it is supported by some 180 Corinthian columns, and twelve suites radiate from the central salon, with its lavish classic décor and romantic atmosphere. These internal rooms range from doubles to luxury suites, and all guests can avail of the hotel's award-winning spa and two excellent restaurants. But the Palais Rhoul has another sublime trick up its sleeve: there are six traditional tents dotted about the vast and verdant gardens. These tents are, in fact, spacious and richly designed secluded suites, and some have working fireplaces, private terraces, and charming indoor pools. The perfect hideaway.

€€€

Route de fès – Km 5 Dar Tounsi, Marrakech 40000
palais-rhoul.com
+212 5243-29494

Riad Al Jazira

Riad Al Jazira brings the idea of a holiday hideaway to
a new level. It is in the Medina, and accessed through a
number of winding lanes and some very low tunnels (if you
call in advance, someone will meet you from your taxi to
help with your bags). On arriving, you will be astounded at
how calm the hotel is; the aesthetic is pared back, bright
and clean, with enough traditional overtones to remind you
that you're in the core of the Medina. There are eighteen
comfortable rooms, a roof terrace where breakfast is
served (other meals are available on request), and an
elegant courtyard. A very reasonable spa and a pool for
cooling off complete this peaceful package.

€

—

8 Derb Mayara, Sidi Ben Sliman, Marrakech 40000
riad-aljazira.com
+212 5244-26463

Riad de Tarabel

The beautiful Riad de Tarabel has only been open since 2007, but with its sophisticated interiors and neutral palette it has a subtle 1930s feel. The riad opened with three rooms, but it has been expanded to ten, ranging across four price levels, from Room to Suite. The owners, French aristocrat Leonard Degoy and his partner Rose Fournier (neither of whom has a background in design), created the entire aesthetic, and their blend of traditional and modern tastes gives the hotel its distinctive atmosphere. There are numerous pleasant seating areas throughout, as well as a heated pool (a spa is to open in 2017). You can arrange to have dinner on site, or enjoy an aperitif in the glasshouse bar before exploring the Dar El Bacha quarter.

€€€

—

8 Derb Sraghna, Quartier Dar El Bacha
riad-de-tarabel.com, Marrakech 40000
+212 5243-91706

Ryad Dyor

Finding the Ryad Dyor involves a long walk through the beautiful alleyways of the Medina, but once there you are close to great restaurants, souks, and other places of interest. The hotel feels intimate and comfortable, and the aesthetic combines traditional style with a clean, modern edge. There are seven rooms, and if you can, get a room on one of the upper floors. While the rooms are not very large, they are very cleverly designed; there is plenty of additional exterior space (including a roof terrace) and the communal areas are beautifully lit by candles at night. With a good spa, hammam, and a cooling pool, this is an extremely good-value option for restful Medina accommodation.

€€

—

1 Driba Jdida, Sidi Ben Slimane, Marrakech 40000
ryaddyor.com
+212 5243-75980

Riad Les Yeux Bleus

The exceedingly pretty Riad Les Yeux Bleus is situated in the lively and scenic quarter of Bab Doukkala, and its location offers guests a great array of options for dining, nightlife and culture. Although it has been in business since 2000, the hotel recently underwent an extensive period of restoration, the motivation for which was to reinterpret classic Moroccan hospitality with a contemporary twist, and this goal has certainly been achieved. Each of the riad's eight bedrooms is decorated in its own style, with unifying elements of traditional pieces contrasted with bold, pop colours. After a tiring day exploring the local alleyways of the Medina, guests can enjoy the charming courtyard, the library, and the spa, before retiring to take in the views from the rooftop bar.

€€

---

7 Derb El Ferrane, Bab Doukkala, Marrakech 40000
marrakech-boutique-riad.com
+212 5243-78161

Riad Snan13

Snan13 is an immaculate and extremely good-value riad
in the Mouassine district of the Medina, which is popular
with discerning travellers to the city. As with many hotels
in the Medina, there is some distance to travel on foot,
but staff will happily help you with your bags. There are
five individually decorated (and individually priced) rooms
in the riad; we love Le Petit Patio, which has a charming
private terrace. The communal rooftop solarium is great
for catching the sun, and offers plenty of shaded areas and
an unheated plunge pool to give you a break from the heat.
Breakfast can be enjoyed on the roof, as can an authentic
local dinner, although a day's notice for the latter is required.

€

—

Mouassine, Derb Snan 13, Marrakech 40030
riadsnan13.com
+212 5243-81997

Royal Mansour

€€€€+

The Royal Mansour Marrakech was commissioned by King Mohammed VI, whose vision was to marry traditional Moroccan style with ultimate luxury, and the result is unquestionably the city's most magnificent hotel. Frequented by stars and global leaders, the hotel comprises fifty-three riads (inspired by North African, Spanish, Portuguese and Moorish architecture) set over one and a half hectares of gardens. Guests can enjoy three lauded restaurants, a number of lounges and bars, a stunning library, and a world-class hammam and spa, complete with its own tea lounge. Everywhere you look there are nods to the country's creativity and craftsmanship. Ultimate luxury doesn't come cheap, of course, but for a special treat the Royal Mansour guarantees an experience you will never forget.

—

Rue Abou Abbas El Sebti, Marrakech 40000
royalmansour.com
+212 5298-08080

La Sultana

La Sultana is a deluxe five-star hotel with twenty-eight rooms
and suites across five riads, each with its own distinct style.
From check-in – conducted in a lounge setting, rather than
across a desk – the feeling of luxury pervades. The hotel has
an excellent boutique, library, gym and spa, and also offers the
services of a tailor and even cookery classes for guests. The
outdoor pool area, located in a red-brick courtyard, is supremely
calm and feels miles from La Sultana's location in the historical
kasbah area. The vast roof gardens, covering all five riads,
offer commanding panoramic views that encompass the Atlas
Mountains and Saadian Tombs, as well as the Medina below;
order a cactus mojito and enjoy the magnificent sunset.

€€€

—

403 Rue de la Kasbah, Marrakech 40000
lasultanahotels.com
+212 5243-88008

La Villa Nomade

Built in the early 1900s in the heart of the Medina, Riad La
Villa Nomade is full of traditional charm. Upon arrival at the
Medina, you are greeted by friendly staff who transport your
bags to the hotel by cart. Behind the riad's heavy wooden door
is a quintessentially Moroccan haven, with a tranquil central
courtyard garden, twelve distinctive rooms, a hammam and
massage, a library, and a roof terrace solarium with a small
pool. The adjoining restaurant is a simple, modern take on
traditional design, and serves good Moroccan meals with
some dashes of international influence. With a variety of
tranquil indoor and outdoor spaces to explore, La Villa Nomade
is a beautiful sanctuary from the heady delights of the souk.

€€

—

7 Derb El Martstane - Bab Tarzout, Zaouia El Abbassia - Marrakech 40000
lavillanomade.com
+212 5243-85010

Villa des Orangers

€€€€

The unassuming entrance to Villa des Orangers opens to present a truly breathtaking space. It was built in the 1930s in the typical riad style, but was remodelled in the late twentieth century and quickly became part of the Relais & Châteaux family of top global hotels, where it has remained ever since. At twenty-seven rooms this is a fairly large riad hotel, but when resting in the shade of its gardens you might feel like the last – and luckiest – person on earth. As a central five-star hotel, the rooms are expensive, but the sense of luxury does extend to unexpected perks, including private airport transfers, breakfast, lunch and unlimited non-alcoholic drinks included in the price of your stay.

6 Rue Sidi Mimoun, Place Ben Tachfine, Marrakech 40000
villadesorangers.com
+212 5243-84638

Shops

ARTC

ARTC is not an easy place to find, but persevering fashion lovers will be well rewarded. Don't be afraid to call for directions, and you will find the atelier inside what looks like an apartment building, simply marked with the number 96. ARTC is the alias of Jerusalem-born designer Artsi Ifrach, who creates one-off pieces that are untethered by trends, gender or commerce. Everything is handmade and tailored to perfection, using vintage fabrics and with many multicultural influences. ARTC's star is on the rise, and his work can be found in exclusive stores in London, New York and Dubai (among others), but nothing can compare with watching him work and observing the creation of a priceless piece that is unique to you.

—

96 Rue Mohamed El Bequal, Gueliz, Marrakech 40000
art-c-fashion.com
+212 5244-30124

Magasin Général

This treasure trove, located in the industrial zone approximately twenty-five minutes from the city centre, is the best place to go for stylish antique furniture and decorative pieces. It was established by Delphine Mottet a few years ago, and her love for her business and the process of curation is very evident. The compact shop is laid out like an old-fashioned general store, and the main focus is on pieces from the late-nineteenth and early twentieth centuries, so as you'd expect there is more than a hint of French influence. Many pieces are sourced from France, Belgium, and England, making Magasin Général extremely popular with locals who want to give their contemporary homes some soul, and with American tourists, many of whom have their purchases shipped home directly.

—

369 Quartier Industriel Sidi Ghanem, Marrakech 40000
magasin-general-marrakech.com
+212 5243-36673

Max & Jan

Max & Jan is an interesting concept store that is extremely modern but still wholly mindful of its roots. One of the few cutting-edge shops in the Medina, it sells contemporary takes on traditional clothes, jewellery, accessories, candles and souvenirs, resulting in an international feeling; indeed this shop would be right at home in Ibiza (where they now have another outlet). Max and Jan hail from Casablanca and Kortrijk, Belgium, respectively, and their motivation is to bring the best young designers and craftspeople in Morocco to new audiences. They are receiving a hugely positive response so far; they have five stores in Morocco, three in Europe, and they are represented in fifty other innovative international boutiques.

—

14 Rue Amsefah, Sidi Abdelaziz, Marrakech 40030
maxandjan.ma
+212 5243-75570

Norya ayroN

Nyora Nemiche's elegant boutique is located on the first floor of the charming Jardin Café (pg. 84), so you have the perfect excuse to combine a relaxing lunch with some retail therapy. Originally from Algeria and inspired by the craft of the Medina locals, Nemiche specialises in bringing traditional attire into the twenty-first century, and her colourful kaftans, punchy capes, and stylish clutch bags are a joy to behold. Her trademarks are bright colours, off-beat prints, and high-end materials, and the prices for her limited-edition pieces are surprisingly reasonable. Although her store opened as recently as 2013, Nemiche's designs have been spotted on a number of international stars, including Kate Moss, Maggie Gyllenhaal and Monica Bellucci – stylish company indeed.

—

32 Route Sidi Abdelaziz, Marrakech 40000
norya-ayron.com
+212 6612-95990

Palais Saadiens

Marrakech's reputation for fabulous textiles is well known, and if you are looking for a traditional Berber, Bedouin or Arab carpet, a visit to Palais Saadiens is a must. The shop is housed in an old palace, and its spacious layout makes it a comfortable environment in which to take your time and explore the stock to find your perfect piece. Each carpet is a unique handmade work of art made from live-sheep's wool and natural vegetable dyes – or rather, two unique pieces of art, as each is reversible, with one side of summer and one for winter. The friendly staff fully expect you to haggle, and will happily arrange to have your carpet shipped to your home.

—

16 rue My Taib Kssour, Marrakech 40000
palais-saadiens.com
+212 5244-45176

Sarah Maj

Young designer Sarah Maj has been creating her vision of 'pret a porter with an original Moroccan touch' since 2009. She made her name in concept stores across Morocco, and further afield in Milan, and her beautiful boutique in the Medina is a welcoming gallery of her elegant and surprisingly affordable pieces. Her designs are graceful and comfortable, with a focus on grown-up sophistication and natural high-quality fabrics that perfectly suit the Marrakech climate but will stand out as special when you bring them home. Maj has an innate understanding of the importance of individuality; she creates limited numbers of each design, adapting the colours and the application of her craftsmanship to ensure that every piece feels unique.

—

88 rue Amsfeh, Sidi Abdelazize, Marrakech 40000
sarahmaj.com
+212 6612-99710

33 rue Majorelle

The two-storey 33 rue Majorelle is a cool concept store showcasing the work of more than ninety designers and craftspeople, across clothing for adults and children, jewellery, toiletries and homewares. It was established by Monique Bresson and Yehia Abdelnour to promote Moroccan talent, and the shop counts among its many fans Princess Lalla Salma, the wife of King Mohammed VI. There are gifts to suit every budget, and plenty of ways to treat yourself; we particularly like the beautiful lambs' leather handbags by local designer M'H (Martine Hellen). There is also a lovely bright snack bar with an on-street terrace, the perfect place to recharge your batteries before more shopping or a visit to the Jardin Majorelle (pg. 102) opposite.

—

33 rue Yves Saint Laurent, Marrakech 40000
33ruemajorelle.com
+212 5243-14195

What to See

Ben Youssef Madrasa

This madrasa was founded in the fourteenth century by the Merenids and rebuilt by the Saadians in the 1560s, who made it the largest in the country at that time. It was used for the study of the Koran until 1960, and in 1982 it was restored and opened to the public. Today, thousands of visitors seek it out for its historical and religious significance, and for its breathtaking architecture. With an abundance of carved cedar wood, patterned tilework and stucco, it's one of the most wonderful examples of Moorish architecture in the world. It's inexpensive to visit (around €2) and as it is accessible only by foot through the maze of the souk, you should check your route in advance.

—

Kaat Benahid, Marrakech 40000
medersa-ben-youssef.com
+212 5244-41893

El Badi Palace

El Badi ('The Incomparable') is a ruined palace that with a little imagination conjures the magnificence of the Kings of Morocco. Construction was completed in 1593, a vast monument to opulence, replete with gold and onyx. It is said that upon its official unveiling a jester joked, 'It will make a magnificent ruin', and today you can visit the serene complex of what remains for just 10 Dhs. A museum shows an unmissable video visualising the palace in its former glory, and for an extra 10 Dhs you can see the minbar, a treasured pulpit from the twelfth century. The ramparts of the palace offer mesmerising views of the Media, the distant Atlas Mountains, and the storks' nests on the rooftops.

—

Ksibat Nhass, Marrakech
+212 5243-78163

Jemaa el-Fnaa

The eleventh-century Jemaa el-Fnaa is the main square and marketplace of Marrakech, and it is a real feast for the senses, bursting with stalls, food, and entertainment. Be vigilant, as there are big crowds, pickpockets and lots of opportunistic pedlars – such as those with monkeys or snakes who will charge for photos (it's generally advised that you enjoy the animals at a distance). We recommend that you go in the evening, when a massive barbeque takes place amidst the chaos. If you find the throng of the square too intense, you can observe from one of the surrounding cafés; we suggest the rooftop terrace of the Café de Paris, where you can order a mint tea and drink in the view.

—

Derb Chtouka, Marrakech 40008
jemaa-el-fna.com

Saadian Tombs

This mausoleum, the work of Sultan Ahmad al-Mansur Eddahbi, holds the tombs of over sixty members of the Saadian dynasty, and many more of their court. Al-Mansur spared no expense in creating this glorious legacy, importing Italian marble and using real gold for the intricate plasterwork. But a few decades after his death in 1603, Alawite Sultan Moulay Ismail had the tombs blocked off to remove his predecessors from public consciousness. For centuries the only access was through a passage in the Kasbah Mosque, until aerial photographs rediscovered them in 1917. They were painstakingly restored and are now open to the public for just 10 Dhs. It's rightfully a popular destination, so very early morning or late afternoon are the best times to visit.

—

Next to Kasbah Mosque, off Rue de la Kasbah, Marrakech
tombeaux-saadiens.com
+212 6272-86740

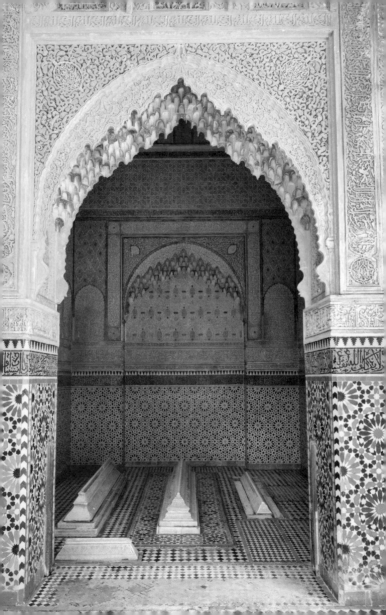

Maison de la Photographie

This small but smart museum is located in a beautiful little riad; it was established in 2009 by Hamid Mergani and Patrick Manac'h, whose mission was to archive and exhibit photographs taken in Marrakech between 1870 and 1960. The resulting collection is a rich and respectful visual history of the city during that period, including photographs, negatives, postcards, and other ephemera, by famous and anonymous photographers alike. The imagery is extremely evocative, and it is fascinating to see what has changed here, and indeed what has changed very little. The museum also boasts a rooftop terrace café with fabulous views of the city and the Atlas Mountains. Open daily from 9.30am to 7pm. Admission is 40 Dhs per adult.

—

46, Rue Souk Ahal Fassi, Marrakech 40000
maisondelaphotographie.ma
+212 5243-85721

Yves Saint Laurent Museum

Work is well underway on the much-anticipated Yves Saint Laurent Museum Marrakech, which is due to open its doors in late 2017. This impressive edifice is located – where else? – on Rue Yves Saint Laurent, beside the designer's treasured Jardin Majorelle (pg. 102), and will house an important edit of his haute couture, sketches, ephemera and personal possessions. Alongside this permanent exhibition, there will be a restaurant, a bookshop and a library. The building's textile-inspired design is the perfect blend of the styles of Saint Laurent and Marrakech, and will be the ideal celebration of his lasting relationship with the city. The Jardin Majorelle is already one of the city's most popular attractions, and this is sure to draw even bigger crowds.

—

Rue Yves Saint Laurent, Marrakech 40000

Restau-
rants

Al Fassia

Al Fassia has been serving delicious food in two locations for thirty years, and this restaurant, in Gueliz, is one of our favourites. Generous portions of freshly prepared traditional dishes are served by a discreet and attentive all-female team – be sure to ask your waitress for her recommendations. Speciality main courses, such as the steamed lamb shoulder or pigeon vermicelli, must be ordered a day in advance, but we recommend the excellent tagines. Vegetarians are also well catered for. Its sterling reputation makes this a very popular spot, so reservations are essential. Al Fassia is open six days a week for lunch and dinner (closed Tuesdays) so you will have ample opportunity to enjoy its authentic cuisine and cosy atmosphere.

€€€

—

55 Boulevard Zerktouni, Marrakech 40000
alfassia.com
+212 5244-34060

Dar Yacout

€€€€

Dar Yacout is tricky to find. It's situated in the Medina, behind an unmarked wooden door, but do everything that you can to find it because it's truly spectacular. When you arrive, head straight for the stunning spiral staircase and climb to the roof terrace to take in the view of the dining area below and the Medina outside. From there, go to the first floor; enjoy a drink and some live music, before taking a seat beside the pool for dinner. A set menu is served, typically Moroccan salad followed by tagines and finally a large traditional cake, and the portions are extremely generous. If you're looking for somewhere memorable and quintessentially 'Marrakech', the palatial Dar Yacout will not disappoint.

—

79 Sidi Ahmed Soussi, Marrakech 40030
daryacout.com
+212 5243-82929

Comptoir Darna

Since its debut in 1999, Comptoir Darna has established itself as a Marrakech institution, and it strikes the perfect balance between old and new. It combines a restaurant and club with live music and dance shows – including belly dancing – making it an ideal venue for groups. Try to ensure that you are seated inside, where crowds of well-dressed locals mingle with tourists, so that you can enjoy the luxe, sexy interiors and lively atmosphere. The extensive menu fuses traditional dishes with modern international influences; the music begins at around 8.30pm, the dancing at 10.30pm, so enjoy a delicious meal before watching the show with a smoked cocktail and enjoying the fun long into the night. Booking is recommended.

€€€€

—

Avenue Echouhada, Hivernage, Marrakech 40000
comptoirmarrakech.com
+212 5244-37702

Foundouk

€€€

Located in a historic building in one of Marrakech's oldest neighbourhoods, Foundouk is a contemporary international restaurant that retains a distinctly Moroccan vibe. The interiors are dark, elegant and cosy, but if you can, try to secure a table on the second-storey terrace, which offers the most gorgeous *al fresco* dining experience. Booking in advance will give you the best chance to get one of these romantic tables overlooking the Medina. The sophisticated menu reflects this fusion of the traditional and the cosmopolitan; expect to find high-quality tagines and pastillas alongside dishes like green pea puree with wasabi, and squid ink tagliatelle. Foundouk is open from 7pm to midnight, Tuesday to Sunday, and bookings can be made through the website.

—

55 Souk Hal Fes, Kaat Bennahid, Marrakech 40000
foundouk.com
+212 5243-78190

Grand Café de la Poste

Entering the Grand Café de la Poste feels like stepping back in time; its elegant décor and its French-infused menu evokes the colonial era like nowhere else. It has been open since 1915 – customers would leave letters here for collection – and in 2005 it reopened after a lengthy period of renovation and refurbishment that restored it to its original glory. The only addition to its original form is the charming, leafy terrace, and seating inside or out is equally enjoyable. It is open from 8am to 1am, making it the perfect place for a coffee, aperitif, lunch or dinner. Try to time your visit for cocktail hour, as they excel in their mixed drinks.

€€€

—

Avenue Imam Malik, Marrakech 40000
facebook.com/legrandcafedelaposte
+212 5244-33038

Kechmara

€€

Kechmara is a lively modern bistro in the Gueliz district that offers all-day dining, moving effortlessly from a bright and airy daytime café to a relaxing dinner destination, and into a buzzing nightspot, with live music during the week. The extensive menu offers light snacks and international mains, with tapas also available in the evenings. The interiors are chic and contemporary; there is art by local artists on display, which changes every three months. The service in Kechmara is exceptionally friendly, and while it is certainly very popular with tourists, it has a local, hipster feel, making it a fun destination for dinner followed by a cold beer or a cocktail on the terrace.

—

3 Rue de la Liberté, Marrakech 40000
kechmara.com
+212 5244-22532

La Paillote

La Paillote is a fairly new restaurant four kilometres from the city centre. The name means 'The Hut', which is a very modest title for this beautiful restaurant. The décor was in part inspired by the film *Out of Africa*, and the feeling, both inside and out, is one of refined, relaxing elegance. It is open from 9am to 10.30pm, and you can have lunch outside in the lush garden, or dinner inside by the soothing open fire. The food is Mediterranean in style, with a focus on high-quality, seasonal ingredients, and the cocktails are extremely good. High ceilings, rich leather and soft lighting make this a warm and inviting environment, with service to match.

€€€€

—

Km 4, route d'Amizmiz, Marrakech 40000
lapaillote.ma
+212 6638-79605

Le Palace

Le Palace is an opulent restaurant, champagne bar
and cocktail club with two very different atmospheres:
downstairs there is a cool candlelit dining room, with plush
red curtains and a dark, sexy atmosphere, and upstairs
has a more brasserie-style feeling. The menu has an
international vibe, with a focus on French and Italian dishes,
and the food is seriously good. DJs play music until 2am,
and every weekend after dinner the space is packed to
capacity with stylish clubbers. While Le Palace is on the
more expensive end of the scale, its old-fashioned glamour
and sumptuous atmosphere is worth the extra cost. Booking
is essential and the dress code is formal.

€€€€

—

Avenue Echouhada, Hivernage, Marrakech 40000
facebook.com/lepalacemarrakech
+212 5244-58902

Le Tobsil

Le Tobsil is a magnificent traditional restaurant in the Medina; as with so many places in this area, it can be a challenge to find, but if you call in advance they will send a member of staff to guide you through the laneways. Le Tobsil serves dinner only, and the set menu, typically featuring generous portions of classics such as tagines, pastillas and pastries, is informed by the day's fresh market produce. Tables, candlelit and strewn with rose petals, are in the alcoves of the house or on the patio under a retractable roof, and dinner is complemented by live music performances every evening. The restaurant is closed on Tuesdays, and booking is essential.

€€€€

—

22 Derb Abdellah Ben Hessein, R'Mila Bab Ksour, Marrakech 40000
+212 5244-44052

Nomad

The trendy Nomad, with its Scandinavian-tinged aesthetic and healthy menu, is *the* place to grab lunch or dinner in the Medina. Located above a tasteful ceramics boutique called Chabi Chic, there is a stylish dining room on the first floor and a spectacular rooftop terrace which overlooks the spice market. The décor is tasteful and elegant, with lively splashes of black and white, and the menu is a similar blend of traditional dishes with modern twists, such as the vegetarian interpretation of the traditional pigeon pastille and lots of locally sourced fish and fresh herbs. Booking is recommended to secure a table on the terrace, where you can watch the sunset over dinner and cocktails.

€€

—

1 Derb Arjaan, just off Rahba Kedima, Marrakech 40000
nomadmarrakech.com
+212 5243-81609

Cafés

Café
Clock

Café Clock is an ideal pit stop as you explore the kasbah. It is housed in an old school and is full of interesting Islamic and Moroccan art (much of it for sale). It also has a wonderful community atmosphere, as diverse crowds gather to participate in a rich calendar of cultural events, including storytelling, dancing, concerts, cooking classes, and crash courses in the local vernacular. Breakfast is served all day, and there is a range of snacks and main dishes that are all very reasonably priced (if you're feeling adventurous you can try their famous camel burger). Take a seat on the roof terrace, order a smoothie or an ice-cream float, and enjoy the infectious, upbeat vibe.

224 Derb Chtouka, Marrakech 40000
marrakech.cafeclock.com
+212 5243-78367

Le Jardin

Although it is tricky to find, Le Jardin is a very popular lunch café with tourists, who seek out its tranquil ambience. Follow your GPS through the souk of the Medina to the crossroads between Dar el Bacha and Riad Laârouss, and you'll come to a beautiful studded wooden door that opens into a delightful courtyard full of palm trees, bamboo and banana leaves. You will also find some unusual inhabitants – the café is home to budgies, little wild birds and a number of ambling turtles. The menu offers a selection of hot and cold plates, and we recommend that you opt for something local. Alcohol is not served, but there is a good range of fresh fruit juices, milkshakes and teas.

—

32 Sidi Abdelaziz, Marrakech 40000
lejardin.ma/en
+212 5243-78295

Terrasse
Des
Épices

Terrasse Des Épices is a simple but extremely reliable café on one of the small squares in the souk. When the weather is very hot, street-level seating is comfortable and offers a great vantage point to observe the traders, but otherwise head directly for the roof terrace, which is particularly charming in the evening, when the earthy tones glow under lanterns. The menu is a blend of traditional Moroccan and international dishes, and their pastries are renowned. The music is cool, the service is professional and courteous, and there are delightful little details such as complimentary straw hats in the heat of day and blankets to keep you warm as you watch the sun go down. Booking is recommended in the evenings.

—

15 Souk Cherifia, Sidi Abdelaziz, Marrakech 40000
terrassedesepices.com
+212 5243-75904

Bars & Clubs

Bô-Zin

Bô-Zin is a glamorous bar and restaurant, located a short taxi ride south of the city centre, that draws a consistently chic crowd. The international menu is good, but for us, Bô-Zin is all about the party atmosphere, particularly Thursday to Sunday, when there are live dance performances. The décor is a blend of traditional Moroccan and French art deco influences, with subtle atmospheric lighting and rich velvets, that then opens up to a large bamboo-lined garden with low-lying sofas, where live DJs play cool chill-out music in the evening that builds after dinner to a crescendo late into the night. An elegant and fun place to spend the evening; dress to impress.

—

Route de l' Ourika Km 3,5, Marrakech 40000
bo-zin.com
+212 5243-88012

Jad Mahal

If you want to let your hair down and dance, especially at the weekend, then Palais Jad Mahal is the place to go. The entrance is immediately striking, as ladies pass by balancing trays of candles on their heads, and the interiors do not disappoint. Built around a central courtyard pond, the venue is lush, candlelit and immediately welcoming. Food is served, but we recommend that you save your money and energy for night-time. For an aperitif or casual drink you can have a seat at the bar; to get a table, a bottle will cost you 1,000 Dhs, but then you can comfortably enjoy the live bands and entertainers – including acrobats and fire-eaters – from midnight to 3am (Tuesday to Sunday). Elegant attire is required.

—

Rue Haroun Errachid, Marrakech 40020
palaisjadmahal.net
+212 5244-36984

Lotus Club

Lotus Club is a well-established cool bar and restaurant in the fashionable Hivernage neighbourhood, adjacent to the Palace Restaurant (pg. 76) and opposite the Comptoir Darna (pg. 66). It is open for dinner from 7.30pm but it is at 10pm that it really comes alive, with belly dancing, followed by African dancers, traditional Moroccan guitar from house musician Mood, then a DJ who spins until 1am. The space is elegant and brooding, with lots of candlelight; to secure the prime tables at the bar you'll have to buy a bottle, costing approximately 1,000 Dhs. If that's beyond your budget, there is still plenty to explore, and in good weather it is hard to beat a cocktail beside the garden pool.

—

Rue Ahmed Chaouqi, Marrakech 40000
lotusclubmarrakech.com
+212 5244-21736

Sky Lounge

The Sky Lounge crests the luxurious Pearl Hotel and is accessible to residents and non-residents alike; enter the opulent lobby and take the elevator to the roof, where you will be met with spectacular views of the city and a truly chilled atmosphere. Reclining on a daybed by the round azure pool at any time of day is infinitely relaxing; you can dine on sushi in the rooftop Namazake restaurant, or simply order a cocktail and enjoy the vibe as the sun sets and the music rises. You can expect to pay a little more for a setting like this, but the crowd is buzzing, the service is good, and you are guaranteed a memorable time. Open daily to 1.30am.

—

Av. Echouhada et Rue du Temple, Hivernage, Marrakech 40000
thepearlmarrakech.com
+212 5244-24242

So Night Lounge

So Night Lounge is a complex which has four distinct spaces for entertainment in the fragrant gardens of the Sofitel Marrakech. Upon arrival you are met with the invigorating smell of fresh citrus from the first space, So Nice terrace, where you can enjoy chilled-out *al fresco* cocktails and shishas. So Good restaurant serves a modern Moroccan menu with French and Asian touches from 7pm until midnight, after which time you can stay for drinks and music. So Zen is a chic VIP area, and finally So Fun club offers live music, DJs and dancing until around 4.30am. Its location means that the crowd is predominantly tourists, particularly in the summer, but it draws a good standard of well-dressed clientele.

—

Rue Haroun Errachid, Hivernage, Marrakech 40000
so-nightlounge.com
+212 6565-15009

Parks

Bahia Palace Gardens

Bahia translates to 'brilliance', and those maintaining this nineteenth-century structure have done an excellent job in preserving the magnificence of the palace and its beautiful gardens, which are both situated in the Medina, along the northern edge of the Jewish quarter. The complex was originally constructed in the 1860s and in keeping with the style of the era, it combines Moroccan and Islamic architecture. The two-acre garden comprises three courtyard spaces, with greenery framing glimpses of the wonderful buildings. We recommend that you go later in the day, when the gardens are cooler and you can admire their gradual transformation in the glow of the setting sun.

Open daily, 8am to 5pm.

---

5 Rue Riad Zitoun el Jdid, Marrakech 40000
palais-bahia.com

Cyber Park

The large, leafy Cyber Park is something of a well-kept secret, particularly amongst the young people of Marrakech, who flock here to use its free Wi-Fi. It is located opposite the Medina Gardens, within the Technology College, but despite these techy connections it is lush, pretty and green, and a lovely place to unwind on hot days. There are further plans to marry the educational and botanical aspects of the park, including the addition of interesting signs on plant species, conservation and the environment. Leave the trappings of the tourist centres behind, and enjoy the cool shade of the orange and olive trees as you watch the local students coming and going and happily working outdoors.

Open daily, 7am to 6pm.

—

Avenue Mohammed VI, Marrakech 40020

Le Jardin Secret

This garden in the heart of the Medina stands on the site of what was the Riad of the Governor of the Medina in the nineteenth century, although its historical significance stretches back to the sixteenth century, when this district was first developed by the Saadian dynasty. A full renovation was completed in 2016, and now the gardens and buildings can be explored by the public. There are two parts: the exotic garden, reflecting the international influences that have permeated Marrakech, and the Islamic garden, which has been designed according to nineteenth-century tastes. Admission is 50 Dhs (children twelve and under go free), and there is a shop and a café.

Open daily, 9.30am to 7pm.

—

184 Rue Mouassine, Marrakech 40000
lejardinsecretmarrakech.com/en
+212 5243-90040

Majorelle Garden

Jacques Majorelle was a French painter who came to Marrakech in 1919 to recuperate from heart problems, and the Majorelle Garden is his enduring masterpiece. The garden is bursting with rare plants but is perhaps best known for the piercing use of blue; this particular tone was inspired by the Atlas Mountains and has since become known as 'Majorelle Blue'. The garden was opened to the public in 1947, and is now one of the country's most popular attractions. In 1980 it was purchased by Yves Saint Laurent to save it from redevelopment; following his death in 2008, his ashes were scattered in the garden. It is open 365 days a year (check the website for seasonal hours) and general admission is 70 Dhs.

Open daily, 8am to 6pm (May to September).

—

Rue Yves Saint Laurent, Marrakech 40000
jardinmajorelle.com
+212 5243-13047

Menara Gardens

Menara Gardens is a vast landscaped area, at the core of which is a large man-made lake that is the terminus for irrigation channels that run from the Atlas Mountains. It is remarkable that this system, which channels water for approximately 30km, is around 700 years old, and it in turn irrigates the some 30,000 olive trees that radiate from it. To walk here takes around forty-five minutes, but if you have access to a car we suggest that you drive and enjoy a short peaceful walk around the garden. Visitors should not come expecting a lush oasis; rather this is a simple, tranquil garden that is popular with local families who come here to picnic and to play.

Open daily, 8am to 6pm.

—

Avenue de la Menara, Marrakech 40000
jardin-menara.com
+212 6155-37266

Check What's On

Biennale
International Film Festival
Theatre Royal

Biennale

Although only founded in 2004, the Marrakech Biennale is now considered to be among the best twenty in the world. The original aim of the festival was to celebrate creativity, embrace diversity and promote understanding, and of course to assert Morocco as a leader in contemporary art. Under the direction of Vanessa Branson and Abel Damoussi, it has grown into a thriving and inclusive event for visual arts and literature. In 2016 they took this one step further, presenting the programme in public spaces completely free of charge, attracting new audiences and further strengthening the festival's relationship with the city. Enthusiasts can also buy VIP passes (€350), which grant access to exclusive events and parties. Check the website for dates and listings.

—

62 rue de Yougoslavie, Gueliz, Marrakech 40000
marrakechbiennale.org
+212 5244-38978

Internat-ional Film Festival

Usually held in early December, Marrakech International Film Festival was created in 2001 by King Mohammed VI to promote the national film industry, and a great deal of effort has been channelled into creating a festival of which the country is very proud. By reaching out to contemporaries, the industry has created strong global ties and reinvigorated the country as a prime filming destination. Industry prizes and celebrity sightings aside, there is a great deal to enjoy during the festival. There are over eighty films screened across four venues, and the most memorable element is the massive nightly open-air screenings in Jemaa el-Fnaa (pg. 54). Visit the website to register for accreditation, which gives access to attend screenings.

—

Various locations
festivalmarrakech.info
+212 5244-32493

Theatre Royal

The design of the Theatre Royal, a subtly modern interpretation of traditional architecture, is the work of the renowned architect Charles Boccara, who hails from Tunisia but has made Marrakech his home. Its construction, which began in the 1970s, is complex and ongoing, but the open-air theatre has been completed and it is here that most events are staged. Inside, the entrance hall and balconies hold regular art exhibitions, but visually the main auditorium steals the show with its dramatic domed ceiling. The majority of performances are in Arabic or French, but the diverse programme of plays, ballet, opera and live music offers much that will not be lost in translation. Ask the staff in your accommodation for up-to-date event listings.

—

Avenue Hassan II, Marrakech 40000
+212 5244-31516

Before you visit Marrakech, you might want to check out these books and films to give you a better sense of the city.

Books

Dreams of Trespass: Tales of a Harem Girlhood
Fatima Mernissi

'When you happen to be trapped powerless behind walls, stuck in a dead-end harem, you dream of escape.' Fatima Mernissi was an academic sociologist and feminist who wrote several books concerning Islam and women's role within it. She was born in a Fez harem in 1940, and *Dreams of Trespass* is her fictive memoir. It is a unique piece of work, telling a Moroccan story from a woman's point of view, and while the central question is the concept of freedom, it powerfully depicts the history and daily life of Morocco.

The Forgiven
Lawrence Osborne

Osborne's best-selling 2012 novel features David and Jo, a wealthy couple

from London who decide to go into the middle of the Moroccan desert for a crazy three-day party. While driving at night, they have a car accident on a desolate road, killing a Muslim fossil seller. They take the body and proceed to their wild and decadent party, and as the story unfolds, the chasm between the locals and these Westerners is rent deeper and deeper. While the characters are less than personable, the descriptive prose of this gripping novel makes it an absorbing, atmospheric read.

The Last Storytellers
Richard Hamilton (Translated by Ahmed Tija)

For thousands of years, Morocco's master storytellers have spun tales of intrigue, love, magic, death and trickery in public squares to awed local audiences, including Marrakech's own

iconic Jemaa el-Fnaa. With this tradition now under threat, BBC journalist Richard Hamilton tracked down the city's last storytellers and recorded their captivating tales for posterity. Luckily for tourists in Marrakech, storytellers still ply their ancient trade in the squares, and the showmanship of the storyteller transcends language barriers – but why not add depth to the experience by reading beforehand some of the tales you might be lucky enough to see told in real life?

Lords of the Atlas: The Rise and Fall of the House of Glaoua
Gavin Maxwell

Gavin Maxwell was a colourful aristocratic naturalist writer from Scotland who travelled to Morocco in 1966, where he traced the rise and fall of the famous Glaoui family, the last rulers of the country under the French. Their story and that of his travels in Morocco was published to some controversy, outlining as it does the often bloody past of the country; it was deemed subversive and subsequently banned from import for many years. This in-depth and illuminating account of a complex time in Morocco's history is not for the faint hearted, but it is rich in detail and atmosphere.

Films

Hideous Kinky
(1998)

Based on a 1992 novel by Esther Freud, this movie tells the story of an Englishwoman called Julia (Kate Winslet) who travels to Morocco in the early 1970s with her two young daughters, in search of herself and spiritual revelation. Told from the perspective of the younger daughter, Lucy, *Hideous Kinky* is a dazzling movie: breathtaking landscapes, romantic adventures, traditional Moroccan music mixed with popular hippy songs, and wonderful acting make this a compelling piece of work.

Lawrence of Arabia
(1962)

Lawrence of Arabia is an unparalleled masterpiece, and certainly one of the greatest films of all time. It is the story of T.E. Lawrence (Peter O'Toole), a British archaeologist and military officer who led the Arab tribes against the Turks in the First World War. At over three hours long it is an epic work of art, depicting not only a significant part of history, but the inner struggles of an ordinary man as he becomes a hero. For first-time visitors to Morocco, where part of the film was shot, *Lawrence of Arabia* is essential viewing.

Mimosas
(2016)

It is the dying wish of an aging sheikh to be buried next to his loved ones in the medieval city of Sijilmasa, and so a caravan sets out to bring him on his final journey through the Atlas Mountains. When the sheikh dies along the way, a young preacher takes command to lead the group on the treacherous road to the deceased's destiny. Aptly described as an 'Eastern western', this moody, minimalist piece grippingly contrasts tradition and modernity, and was the deserving winner of the Grand Prize at Cannes's *Semaine de la Critique*.

The Wind and the Lion
(1975)

Set at the turn of the twentieth century, *The Wind and the Lion* is based on the real-life Perdicaris kidnapping that sparked an international incident in 1904. In the movie, a young American widow and her children are abducted by a Berber chieftain, Raisuli (Sean Connery), prompting the US President Theodore Roosevelt to intervene and send a rescue mission to Morocco. A complex relationship develops between Raisuli and the widow, pushing the theme of America's emergence as a world power into the background.

Check out these sites and accounts for the most up-do-date events and insights into Marrakech life:

Influencers

Ali Berrada
instagram.com/ali_berrada

Berrada's stunning photographs of his native Morocco and beyond are sure to inspire.

Bewildered in Morocco
bewilderedinmorocco.com

This slick blog is the work of Monika, a Polish woman who made Morocco her home in 2013. She offers travel tips and info for tourists, expats, business travellers and Moroccans.

Humans of Morocco
instagram.com/ humansofmorocco

Illuminating photographic project with the mission of shedding more light on the ethnic, cultural Moroccan population.

Made in Marrakech
madeinmarrakech.co.uk

One-stop-shop for cultural events listings and for dining, nightlife and shopping news.

Maroc Mama
marocmama.com

A visually pleasing site by Amanda, a mother of a Moroccan–American family in Marrakech. Originally a food blog, it has grown to incorporate great tips for visitors to the city.

Maryam Montague
mmontague.com

A creative and varied blog by Maryam Montague, an American designer, hotelier and humanitarian based in Marrakech.

Much Morocco
muchmorocco.com

This resource for visitors to Morocco is particularly strong on outdoor activities, such as golf, cycling and kayaking, in and around Marrakech.

Tips from the inside: we asked some top Marrakech creatives for their favourite spots

Contributors

Yannick Alléno
yannick-alleno.com

Yannick Alléno is one of the world's top chefs, having been awarded six Michelin stars during his illustrious career. Based in his native France, in 2008 he established a new company to expand his reach to the best global hotels. In 2009 he took control of the three restaurants of the Royal Mansour, Marrakech (pg. 32).

'I'm extremely proud of the Grande Table Marocaine at the Royal Mansour; it combines tradition and innovation, offering rich, respected Moroccan classics filtered through our sincere vision for modern cuisine. The menu is the result of a long and rigorous period of research that gave us a full understanding of the local traditions, ancestral know-how and singular resources of this wonderful cuisine. I also highly recommend the new pool at the Royal Mansour; it is elegant, stylish, and extremely relaxing.

'I am a fan of La Maison de la Photographie (pg. 58), and the contemporary art collection at Musée de Marrakech (museedemarrakech.ma). Also worth a look is Le Jardin Anima (anima-garden.com) by André Heller – it's an incredible place and its colours make me happy.

'Seek out the workshop and gallery of Yahya (yahya-group.com), a respected artist who designs lighting, furniture, accessories, decorative pieces, architectural elements and artworks. His aesthetic is contemporary and ultra-chic whilst being infused with delicate oriental touches.

'At night, I'm a fan of the festive atmosphere, great cocktails and good music at Buddha Bar (buddhabar.ma)'

Mohamed Amine Kabbaj
marrakechbiennale.org

Born in Casablanca, architect Mohamed Amine Kabbaj has been working in Marrakech since 1980. He is a keen art collector and an accomplished curator, and is the current President Executif of the Marrakech Biennale (pg. 108).

'I love to wander through Souk Semmarine, the main thoroughfare in the Medina, where the shops are plentiful. Handwoven blankets hang alongside locally dyed and produced leather bags. Artisanal products from across Morocco – thuya wood, babouche slippers, carpets in all styles – and even imports from around the world are for sale behind the most unassuming shopfronts.

'When I've had enough of shopping, I like to have lunch or dinner on one of the many rooftop terraces, with views of the city and the snowy Atlas Mountains in winter. Le Grand Café de la Poste (pg. 70) was originally built as the post office, as the name suggests, in the early 1900s. Today it is a charming restaurant tastefully decorated in a colonial style and one of my favourite places to have dinner, coffee in the morning, or to meet with colleagues and friends.

'Marrakech has many art galleries, including David Bloch Gallery (davidblochgallery.com), Galerie 127 (galerienathalielocatelli.com) in Gueliz, and Le 18 (le18.weebly.com) in the Medina. It's also worth visiting the Al Maaden Museum of African Contemporary Art (macaal.org) in the Palmeraie.

'The École Supérieure des Arts Visuels de Marrakech (ESAV, esavmarrakech.com) is not only a modern audio and visual arts school, but a leading cultural centre. They regularly host art exhibitions, film screenings and conferences that are open to the public. ESAV is also connected to Dar Bellarj (darbellarj.com) in the Medina, which is another important cultural space that hosts exhibitions, cultural events and musical evenings.'

Vanessa Branson
el-fenn.com

Entrepreneur, campaigner and curator Vanessa Branson co-owns El Fenn, a stunning boutique hotel in the Medina that combines traditional luxury and modern style. A keen collector of contemporary art, in 2005 Branson founded the Marrakech Biennale (pg. 108) which has become a hugely significant part of the country's cultural calendar.

'I'm obviously biased, but when it comes to restaurants I think that El Fenn's chef and menus are pretty exemplary!

'I always enjoy Al Fassia, too – it's a restaurant owned and run by women at 55 Boulevard Mohamed Zerktouni (pg. 64).

'These days, I don't tend to frequent the city's bars – I'm more of a daytime lady now – but for a day by the pool Beldi Country Club (beldicountryclub.com) never fails to please. The pool is fresh, long and elegant, and is surrounded by ancient olives. Having lunch under the trees surrounded by roses is a real pleasure.

'I also highly recommend a visit to Maison Tiskiwin (tiskiwin.com), which houses the unique collection of Dutch anthropologist Bert Flint. You can view his wonderful artefacts, ranging from Tuareg camel saddles to beautiful High Atlas carpets, all labelled with Bert's eccentric text.'

Aurore Chaffangeon
madameamarrakech.com

Journalist and Publishing Director Aurore Chaffangeon arrived in Morocco in 1998 and never left. She worked as editor-in-chief on a number of magazines, before establishing her own publication, *Madame in Marrakech*, a bimonthly magazine that explores the best places in the city to eat, party, shop, and generally treat yourself.

'Located an hour from Marrakech, in the heart of a twenty-two hectare garden, is the beautiful Domaine de la Roseraie (la-roseraiehotel.com). The ground-floor rooms and suites open out onto thousands of roses, centuries-old olive trees, giant agaves and oversized magnolia. The hotel was created about forty years ago by hospitality pioneer Abdelkader Fenjiro, and it has since welcomed royalty and celebrities, who come to enjoy the peaceful seclusion.

'Jardin Rouge (montresso.com) is the name on all art lovers' lips these days. This artists' village, created by the Montresso Foundation, is located approximately twenty kilometres from the city, and is certainly worth visiting. Art is everywhere – on the walls, on the ceilings, in the garden – and it has just inaugurated an exhibition space of 1,300 m^2.

'For shopping, I love Art Ouarzazate (facebook.com/artouarzazatea). Designer Samad is simply a genius; using furs recovered from the wardrobes of grandmothers, canvas and precious fabrics, he reimagines apparel and accessories in a way that is ultra-original, with a hint of Eastern influence.

'The Palais Soleiman (palais-soleiman.com) is my favourite restaurant. The palace dates from the nineteenth-century, and the atmosphere is chic and relaxed, with carved ceilings, frescoes, Baccarat chandeliers, Napoleon III armchairs, and art deco tables. The bar of the Selman Marrakech (selman-marrakech.com) has a unique atmosphere. It was beautifully designed by Jacques Garcia, but its special charm comes from the thoroughbred horses that the owner breeds here. Guests can enjoy a drink by the pool and watch the horses roaming the grounds.'

Hassan Hajjaj
taymourgrahne.com/artists/hassan-hajjaj

Hassan Hajjaj is a hugely versatile artist whose vibrant catalogue incorporates photography, installation art, performance, fashion and interior design. Often referred to as 'the Andy Warhol of Marrakech', he divides his time between there and London, and his work is held in numerous prestigious international collections.

'My favourite places to eat in Marrakech are Nomad (pg. 78) and the Amal Association (facebook.com/AmalNonProfit), a non-profit culinary training centre that supports under-privileged women in the city. For night-time, I enjoy Comptoir Darna (pg. 66), and my favourite shop is, of course, Riad Yima (riadyima.com) [Riad Yima is Hassan Hajjaj's gallery and boutique].

'In Marrakech we are spoiled with great places; some of the best are 127 Gallery, Jardin Majorelle, Le Jardin Des Arts, Restaurant Rahba Lakdima, Riad El Fenn, Dar Charifa, Dar Bellarj Foundation, and the Atlas Mountains.'

Artsi Ifrach
art-c-fashion.com

Artsi Ifrach is a leading fashion designer who turns vintage Moroccan textiles into haute couture under his label ARTC. His pieces are available in exclusive stores around the world, and fashion fans can visit his stylish Marrakech atelier to peruse his pieces and watch him work (pg. 42).

'Nomad is my favourite restaurant in Marrakech, for many reasons, prime among them the cool atmosphere and good food.

'For a great night out, I recommend Comptoir Darna. I love the oriental style, and a night spent there always creates fond memories.

'33 rue Majorelle (pg. 48) has an excellent range of eclectic Moroccan-design pieces in all fields, and if you're looking for carpets, head for Sufian Carpets in the Medina, where you will find the most exclusive and traditional examples.

'If you're spending a day in the Medina, be sure to take in Riad 18 (le18.weebly.com). This is a really exciting cultural centre that was established by young Moroccan photographer Laila Hida, and it's wonder-

Photography Credits

Pg. 6 Conor Clinch, Pg.8 shutterstock/Maurizio De Mattei, Pg.13 Riad Snan13, Pg.14 La Sultana, Pg.16 Amanjena, Daniel Herendi, Pg.18 Dar Seven, Pg.19 Dar Seven, Pg.20 Ksar Char-Bagh, Bernardo Ricci Armani, Pg.22 Palais Rhoul, Pg.23 Riad Al Jazira, Pg.24 Riad de Tarabel, Yves Duronsoy, Pg.25 Riad de Tarabel, Yves Duronsoy, Pg.26 Ryad Dyor, Pg.27 Ryad Dyor, Pg.28 Riad Les Yeux Bleus, Pg.29 Riad Les Yeux Bleus, Pg.30 Riad Snan13, Pg.31 Riad Snan13, Pg.32 Royal Mansour, Pg.34 La Sultana, Pg.35 La Sultana, Pg.36 La Villa Nomade, Pg.37 La Villa Nomade, Pg.38 Villa des Orangers, Pg.39 Villa des Orangers, Pg.40 33 rue Majorelle, Pg.42 ARTC, Pg.43 Magasin Général, Pg.44 Max & Jan, Pg.45 Norya ayroN, Pg.46 SuperStock/Alamy Stock Photo, Pg.47 Sarah Maj, Pg.48 33 rue Majorelle, Simon Saliot, Pg.50 Riad Snan13, Pg.52 shutterstock/worker, Pg.53 shutterstock/LongJon, Pg.54 shutterstock/ TDway Pg.56 shutterstock/posztos, Pg.57 shutterstock/Jose Ignacio Soto, Pg.58 Maison de la Photographie, Pg.59 Maison de la Photographie, Pg.60 Getty Images/Horst P. Horst/Contributor, Pg.62 Le Palace, Saad Alami, Pg.64 Al Fassia, Pg.65 Dar Yacout, Alan Keohane Pg.66 Comptoir Darna, Andreas Holm, Pg.67 Comptoir Darna, Pg.68 Foundouk, Pg.69 Foundouk, Pg.70 Grand Café de la Poste, Pg.71 Grand Café de la Poste, Pg.72 Kechmara, Pg.74 La Paillote, Pg.75 La Paillote, Alexandre Chaplier, Pg.76 Le Palace, Saad Alami, Pg.77 Le Tobsil, Pg.78 Nomad, Pg.79 Nomad, Pg.80 rbeverson, Pg.82 Café Clock, Azeddine Maizi, Pg.83 Extrablatt, Reg Marjason, Pg.84 Le Jardin, rbeverson, Pg.85 Le Jardin, rbeverson, Pg.86 Terrace des Épices, Pg.88 Royal Mansour, Pg.90 Bô-Zin, Pg.92 Jad Mahal, Pg.93 Lotus Club, Pg.94 Sky Lounge, Leonardo, Pg.95 So Night Lounge. Zoubir Benali, Pg.96 Le Jardin Secret, Pg.98 shutterstock/saiko3p, Pg.99 Getty Images/Lonely Planet, Pg.100 Le Jardin Secret, Pg.101 Le Jardin Secret, Pg.102 shutterstock/saiko3p, Pg.104 Christine Wehrmeier/ Alamy Stock Photo, Pg.106 Le Jardin Secret, Pg.108 Fatiha Zemmouri, Pg.110 Getty Images/ Abdelhak Senna/Staff, Pg.112 shutterstock/Philip Lange, Pg.114 shutterstock/Gary Yim